D1709942

On the Way to the Paintings of Forest Robberies

ON THE WAY TO THE PAINTINGS OF FOREST ROBBERIES

Jennifer Nelson

Fence Books
Astoria, New York 2025

FENCE B⋺OKS

On the Way to the Paintings of Forest Robberies, 2025
Copyright © 2025 Jennifer Nelson

Cover image by the author and designer, based on etchings by
Pieter Molijn and by Bastiaen Stopendael after Cornelis Visscher (II) after
Pieter Bodding van Laer made available by the Rijksmuseum, Amsterdam.

The Ottoline Prize

Published in the United States by
Fence Books
36-09 28th Avenue, Apartment 3R
Astoria, NY 11103-4518

www.fenceportal.org

This book was printed at Versa Press
Fence Books are distributed by Consortium Book Sales and Distribution
Book design by Sharon DeGraw

Library of Congress Control Number: 2024947576
ISBN 13: 9798989978519

First Edition
First Printing
10 9 8 7 6 5 4 3 2

On the Way to the Paintings of Forest Robberies

Sonnet

I will walk again in the primordial
forest: on repeat, to keep it primordial,
because in the beginning
forest is chorus. How much more singing

till I meet my good spouse Death?
When, when I say Death,
will I finally speak of my full self,
a unison of bots?

This is the rule of ghosts. They endure
as much as they're remembered
and carry loss like a song.

This is the loam on the forest floor,
the ongoing of the unremembered
and those remembered wrong.

Contents

Sonnet

Tenure Dossier

Condition for Retention

I don't want to be the cardinal
on which the revolution hangs,
who brightens the winter tree.

I want sufficient sun
to watch shadows change.
I want to turn away from death

and live it another way,
aloft, my guts
metaphorizing pleasure

as I bake my grief above.
Tired oven mind.
The calrods swerve

a second sun. Do not put my name
in the essay on the cult of ends.
I will miss our words when we've won.

CV

Sad master of time, I said to her, even though
I was looking at the trees I had predicted
would bloom unevenly bloom unevenly and not
at her, why when you first come to a place
do you have to imagine where the sun will move
as the months move the Earth — why
do you have to be so right and yet surprised
when the light does things you couldn't predict
to your body? And I don't think she answered

; another person did. Look, there's nothing wrong
with loving melancholy, said this person,
very much looking inside me, as if it were true
that a person were located inside their body,
looking very hard inside me trying
to keep me open, Why are you so afraid
of loving failure, loving loss, if you know the opposite's
bad cheer — and before I knew it they
were hugging me from the inside, which
turns out does not feel like a hug but does

feel like being in one's body: I was proud
of having pulled this great interlocutor out
and to be hugged by them. The sun began to set
and I said, I know you're proud

I won't believe in targets. Arrows
seem pitiful to me. And they laughed at that.

But my sad friend wanted the afterimage talk.
It's not that I'm stupid, she finally said. You can't
be stupid and master time, we agreed
at the same time. She said we'd never see
the same thing twice so she wanted to remark each one
to use it and keep use different from grief.

The dust around me grew brightest as the sun
disappeared. I wanted to give us better names.
I asked my friends who are always with me
what my name was to them. One of us smiled
for the rest. Then someone said, You'd have to
abolish time, which would mean to abolish
use. Where is this realm beyond use? I said.

I don't know, I said. I dream like moss at night.
To know your own name is not
enough. The one who remembers our names
must stay most asleep. Watch
the way a person contorts and you can see
the shape of what they keep under.

Statement of Future Research Plans

At some point the ghosts
stopped being a harem.
I never stopped the sacred dance.
I strung up the fight cage
with chains of the small
flowers that surprise me
every summer growing
on broccoli in the terrible
stores. I watched my sweat
destroy the floors. I poured oil
in each hole, bridegroom
and screen like the moon.

But the ghosts know I'm gone
beyond haunting. In the intertidal
zone, surf, addicted
to loss, my remains perform my ritual.

And they come out of respect for that,
the ghosts.
They hide their arguments in train-runs
and rain.

Please surrect that person, say the ghosts,
correctly, to the priests.
They never had a living master.
Since they know I keep nothing, I am safe,
like a Dante who won't leave hell.
All night long, trains and rain,
all day long, sweat and flowers.

Condition for Retention
for Florence, for Jean

I know I am a ghost to you,
suspended between books.

Children have shrunk
to make me appear.

Even the ink
was siphoned from trees.

What is the point of rehearsing death.
Today I have to tell Florence I'm sorry.

But I am not sorry.
I want Florence to be free.

I want care as an island
with many bridges

or maybe the middle of a frozen lake.
I will wheel you out there.

Or I will have to be the ghost
who laces your feet,

sharpens your skates,
slides you over the ice.

Statement of Future Research Plans

No one's in their body same
as anyone else's being
in their body. I'm not

for disembodiment per se, I'd rather
hold frostbitten
fingers to your throat. I keep the toes

I've lost in a perpetual stew
simmering since the 1520s.
The main perpetuating force

is anger at the narrowness
of what counts as a need.
I will stretch like a prairie

if I must be stranded in the terrible
ruins of a prairie.
In the prairie every

word is attested only once
and changes like a body,
rippling. Sometimes deer

shrug ticks onto leaves
and that is the right kind of attention.
Or at a cold glass apartment wall

a crow seizes up in the sky,
triples in size, and answers,
one intruder to another.

Optional Statement on "Engaging with Diverse Communities"

The origin of dreams,
a spindly fairy
with sharp teeth
whose body is one long iris
flashes at the forest edge.

How can she do it,
not harm the others.
So charged with green.   *Hildegard's viridity*
You have to let me save her. Survival

is love. I have never
stopped asking
to be good. Waking
shows the gulf
inside the asking.

That is the location
of the party
called Survival Is Love.
Dancing on the sandstone
forest embankments
I mark the trees.

Condition for Retention

I don't want to know what sings
in the museum. What is there in art
but more murder, more grief, a fleck

of lapis in the eye
of a laser. The most transgressive
beauty might
end like dawn

this long death, but I
haven't seen it in so long.

The one swan
alive for miles of winter
hoards the only break
where river falls into ice.

There's nowhere left for fun.
I have gone beyond art's time machine
in the land of unforgiveness.
Fuck your cold

therapy. I will not celebrate
pain like a flower. In this museum
I brought a knife
to sabotage the famous
triumph of death.

Writing Sample: The Boxer Codex

The braided blue hair of the sea weaves wide and indefinitely. On it like pointed beads
small ships, bangkas, carry naked natives and the things they have to sell. Seventy years before, Magellan
fucked up a conversation and for another hundred years from here these people were called "thieves,"
ladrones, before their name improved to Spanish slang for "leg of pork." From the image I guess
it was the smoothness and the brownness of their bodies that produced that name, right
or wrong. I myself have looked like a lechon. At first from the roundness of the chests
I assumed these were understood as women on the woven sea, offering fish and fruits, and now suspect
they're often men, but look the same as women, same hair, same no-covering, same roundness all around.
Same face. So, too, the Spanish in the galleon share a face. Across those faces and that braided sea, striations
as from pregnancy or broken tv interrupt, scrolling along the scene. Or single-portion yellowed rain
on selected persons. If you hold the manuscript you see the scene's a fold-out,
the only one, that it has many times been folded, protected, kept vivid. Hence lines. The greatest
saturation is in the dyes of Spanish clothes, which must have seemed exotic, still, a little, to the artist,
given that the artist knew to make the ocean a rhythm of gradient yarns of sea, and the sails of coconut matting
like a checkerboard or basket. No European would have painted those sails, or if they had, they might have made them
look more functional, as a later picture engraved for the Dutch shows CHamoru expert sailors arriving en masse
and getting blown up. But mostly the tell is the sea. This is an East Asian sea, between Ma Yuan's style,
Muromachi painted scrolls, pre-Mughal manuscripts, and early Ming blue-and-white bowls.
Why write an essay here. For the first time I notice a bundle of rods like a fasces
dim in the sea, against its weave, and a CHamoru person diving after: this is iron, the only good
CHamoru people wanted from the Spanish, the point of the coconuts, the water gourds, the fish, the thing
that's most amusing to the profiteers: the different market, that a stupid knife would fetch more goods than gold,
that any weight of iron was worth whole contents of CHamoru boats. How intriguing that they bite

the ropes that grip the iron, "como si fuese un rábano," as if it were a radish and with relish

tie the reciprocal coconut up. At the top of all of this, interrupted by the puny

Cross of Burgundy — red cross on white, what you think of as "Spanish" — which flies at the main and fore

topmasts, runs a flora and fauna margin, semi-repeating, though the bees and birds face the crosses symmetrically

close enough to peck. These ornamental borders come from made-for-export Chinese wares, though in this particular

fake picture book of life on Earth the expectation is to document what's local while demonstrating how

the local color sings, especially the gold, especially extravagant to use it only in the margin

for the edges of petals and parts of bees, outlining a red the way that "Oriental"

restaurants continue this décor. I mean mainly Chinese and Thai American. And this Manila galleon

folded out on the first page, with its relations to the friendly locals, greeting their lightly laden outrigger canoes,

is one reason some people use this word "American" to mean huge occupied swathes of land. The ropes

that reel in coconuts and fling out cords of iron feel inexorable as rhumb lines on a portolan,

deployed everywhere along the coasts, catch everything, catch what's offered and web it.

So I of course enjoy the bite, shown here on the left as if a bite into iron itself,

and on the right as a severing chew before reciprocation. During this exchange the cannons

of the galleon stay quiet, though one threatens foreshortened like a button whoever opens this book.

Are you still in this open-sea market, are you biting the iron hook?

The borders continue more regularly for study pictures of "Ladrones." A spear
comes out from behind one border, peeks across the left, a gimmick
that the girl (?) might jump out of the page. Across the opening her (?) partner
with the topknot hair and bow and 'stache looks ready to kill the Dinagat rat
in the border corner. This rat is now almost extinct, not that rats come first
in mourning. With the "Cagayanes" you get more gold, a hot midriff on her,
literal idols crowning him. If I continue with this sequence I'll repeat this
bad anthropology, attributes, sex, and names. In last night's dream the editor

Gib Var
would not approve my plan

meaning somewhere in me an explorer held back at Gibraltar
wants to make the pictures, commission more. Why else
are there blank pages. If I were emperor!
Here the borders shift from jungle rats to lobster
for "Zambales." Butterflies green
and maize pinned with gold
look in at the corners:

                              what would I do otherwise? If I
led the expedition, should I not
abolish expeditions, should I not yell
at the pictures themselves? "The people of this land
never had a king, and neither did their ancestors."

Martha's texting me about the plague
the way I texted her about the fire.

In *Afterearth*, directed
by Jess X. Snow, Isabella Borgeson
sets several tiny boats
first in the California desert
then in the Pacific
in 2017 or earlier

"there are still boats buried
in this sand" a vision
of a "holy ocean"
after the typhoon
and a double meaning
the word *barcada*
friend-group and boat
or friend/ship
as she swims with hazelgreen eyes
underwater with a candle

reminds me to tell you
barangays still exist
each polity a sailboat
and community at once

these barangays
allied together
sometimes with a raja
or sultan or not
within this continuous sea

which vanishes in the Boxer Codex
after that first scene
but is implied everywhere,
a water way between borders,
sea air in the ink:
an ocean blue seeps through and rules
the empty pages. The gray

of the cannons returns late
in the skin of a Chinese deity
who is our counterpart, a general who records
all people and their names and deeds
and punishes the bad,

and carries through the monsters

gridded up as the book winds down. Of course monsters. You would expect these Europeans
to stop the show with unknown beasts, chimeric parts, a small tusked horse with fire
blitzing from its limbs, a topknotted tiger with five tails, where a stain
looks like it breaks wind. The snowcat has the haircut of native women two
hundred pages back. I could go on: a bunny and elephant square off in size while a dragon
and a "qiirin" prance, their rainbow scales and hair ablaze. But no, the pictures end with birds

shown here as meticulously
as birders might today demand. At least one, "emco," I could confirm in life
by purchasing. In the light of this day in a beplagued
Wisconsin October

I could order a macaw that looks like Emco
from the Pet World Warehouse Outlet
fourteen minutes' drive away, though this facsimile creature
came from Brazil. The only Asian parakeet I could acquire
is the Alexandrine bird, really named after that Alexander,
who probably really had such a pet. They can live thirty years in a cage

and forever in mosaic, as the one from Pergamon
now installed in a museum sanctum in Berlin.
I remember Gib Var hunching over a desk
in those yellow museum backroom lights
consulting the maps, the ones he had
and those to come, in a study room
where nothing had ever lived
except in representation,
spread out on a table,

which is always also an altar.
In that parade of knowledge
offered dead (perhaps to the gray
Warlord of Heaven) I could have no place.

As I woke up I was wondering whether
I could appeal for a second review.
I am a scholar through and through.
The part of me still waking up is asking
Appeal to who? Give me the last word,

poor immortal crane crouched "ho."
Dāndǐng hè, red-crowned crane,

leads a hermit along an edge of the air
as a lost ridge curves

in a scratched-up mirror-sized patch of silk

sometime in the thirteenth century
washed by Ma Yuan
whose studies of water passed on
through the Ma-Xia school
and into woodcuts from the Ming
so the unknown artist of the Boxer Codex

could rework that old insight into water
as a gradient twisting through itself
more than three hundred years later.

The crane is wet. It airs
its butt. Behind it
the last few pages
of the codex chip
paper fragments
out. Beneath its beak
a wormhole flakes
and only stops

when Boxer, British spy, inserts other pages
for context in 1950, that is, another
1590s scribe is made to interrupt

with the local bishop's letters
to the king of Spain and others
describing the need for governance

and conquista. No, the crane couldn't
be a portal. No, there is no door.
I await the verdict
through the accurate
tongue of the last bird,
who has no reader.

Condition for Retention

Today the sun
feels like such a gift the idea
we only roll around it
means all gifts
are self to self.

Ear to wrist: blood
must grunt all day
or relax when no one listens.

I keep beating the ground
to distribute what it saved
from the thunder.

Ekphrases

Frontispiece

I'm not ready to pass through the arch
if to pass through the arch
commits me
to words. Supremacy's
binary, print and white. In the center
at the edge of the arch
is the head of someone not
human, there
to trip humans. Gate
keeper, donkey ears, puzzle, rebus, mix. Eyes
that only stare.
A parted muzzle:

      And because I chimera
am sworn to complain
as the witness of all sides,

      because a disembodied head
      lacks hands,
      the vaulting
      looks like teeth,

and the white where words appear
whips stipple out of stone,
that is, there is
no passage anyway,
at that point I start whistling.

Ovid 1.9 [non bene iunctarum discordia semina rerum]

So there was chaos and discord at the start of creation. Have Actaeon's dogs
ripped him up yet, here in his bunched-
up riding pants, the spurs
still clipped to his boots? No,
a few drops of vermilion
near the top dog's teeth,
else unbroken. Reverse

baptism, splash it left,
            divine female ejaculation
Diana arcs
water up: this
is pleasure, eyes dark, lips
apart, strawberries pluckable
near the edge. Front

and center a naked nymph
splits her legs on the foremost
edge of the panel. Pubic
curls pull hairs from brush. The pleasure
men take in knowing their harm, the pleasure
of going back to beast
gnawed by one's own

beasts, so on: it's a fantasy
to return to conditions of creation, to the original
causes of things joined wrong, disharmony. The order
of being only human
is unnatural at best. If
we transgress, we think, we might
escape. It's autumn, and the leaves give up. Men
keep turning to metamorphosis
by violence, as if force

alone could break the curse. We could
enjoy it, splitting him up
as leaves flee from twigs. His open snout
would gargle spray,
stagpoints sprouted
from his head, the route of tears
charcoaled long, a wrong preorbital

gland. The former beard beshags the throat
where dogs bay out post-bite.... Outside
the painting, scrabbling leaves
click in the trees. I would like
to end this dream. The world is dying,

and I would rather bathe in the disorganized
paint that clumps into discorded seeds,
not well mixed together, a dangerous
pornography, by which I mean a form
that destroys function. Refuses return,
refuses the future. Unburns.

Danaë Danaë Revolution

There's a trick, the trick that men
can use, the flip,
desire desires,
the gold wants me. Every time

I see that nude laid out, that same
pale body touched with blood
beneath, that butchery blush, it's
the window

of coherence, growing
shorter each time
I repeat. I'm only as me
as the last attempt. The more

I see my body the less I'm inside it,
my feet dumb small, my hands
rubescent and genital.

Foolish Argives
and your misuse of prophecy!

There's a version of the story where I want it,
the moment when sun
hits the skylight of my cell,

turns to literal material gold,
and desire desires,
the gold wants me.

That is, I'm the one
who shapes its killing
technology
in honor of the world.

The Prize of Québec

In this world the dead
are labeled "victory."
The dead and one
upright man akimbo and another
releasing a bayonet and what
looks like a small grenade.

Scholars misinterpret
images for a living, call them
worlds, a synecdoche
based on faith in the moment
of creation. Here triple pairs
of caption-clouds, "French regulars" "Canadians"
"and Indians," yield
to red. Even the wind

blows against Québec.
Where I am from in part. I remember
scaling the cliffs of Monterey
and telling K-Sue in almost real time
the moment I knew my ancestors
had taken both sides of big harm. The narrows

here are invisible, the river one-sided
as a lake. Three hundred years ago
the smoke was erased. The general's
assistant sketching wasn't
trying to be right, just
mechanical with organized
death. How to signal victory. Dawn
like a couch on the horizon
and very few
blobs of smoke. Clear
lines of men and ships
have passed the night
in relative silence. The moon
according to Google
had just entered its last quarter, so
the boats must have come
in near total darkness,
elided here for relentless dawn,
the divan. But really

that's what the killers would remember:
the quarter sliver of the moon
glancing off the dark

meniscus of the river, the sweat
in the black-red wool
stuffing the boats, and the dim
occasional torches of this Québec,
which they would end.
After the smoke that looks so moderate here
but was probably actually choking, long after
hearing the general had died, sometimes
at night the soldiers would think
of those hard hours
of clarity, rowing
against the water
against a tiny moon
that is still there almost beside the world, precisely
not watching
whenever we look. On it
ruined flags point back at us.

Don't Kill Yourself

Every observation transforms and fixes, time
is made out of observations, I will kill myself.

The dying cat is clawing a carpet, and I swore
I would always see beauty in the garbage, I

will kill myself, rather than touch the world
and feel my constant harm on it, my pride

like a baseball bat, I'll kill myself. How could I
judge anyone, they are part of the world,

and every time I lecture your heart open
to these early unforested drawings of stags

and the soft shading of their veins, their interior
forests, unpixellating as I reinforce their world,

their reach toward the ancient secret of another life
in charcoal on cloth scraps, I know it won't counter-

balance myself, interruption, broken
highway in a bad dream, I will kill myself,

I think as I erode, bad road. Too much pressure
to serve a smooth escape. I look up *bitumen*

and every time I open my mouth it pours
bright tar, history's required lie about beauty.

The real historical Pisanello confirms his hand,
and then that hand self-sepulchers, tapping

like a one-toned xylophone, osteophone,
that is my music, a parade of single tones

without echo. Toothless wagon-ruts roll
into a slow sea with the moon's percussion.

Burn the Banner of the King

after David Jones

I want to wake up in this gray valley
beneath its well-stripped trees
and join you in the hunt
to burn the banner of the king. Isn't this how
to be kind
while destroying everything?
Let us unmake Christendom together.
The hunting horn that raises the dead
lies across a strong white rill
with orator robes and animal skins beneath it.

If we leave this wood
we leave the join
of nature and messiah. We'd get away
beneath these rusty leaves, but
at what cost? Hard to believe

the war is done while making
war. Why not try to face
what the drawing faces. So we can
grieve together our bad dream. I will break
the horn. You unwind
the ribbons from the tree.

The Last Supper, Designed by Bernaert van Orley, at the Met

This is the most devastating Christ, eyes
split, one dull
and damaged, the other
sharp almost at you and then
away: your own
self-hatred in that vacancy, his upper lip
so dark it looks from far
away like he's speaking.
But if he spoke it would be speech
without content, a discontent,
since if you channel God
no one will be happy,
since you aren't God, but a person,
and persons require freight. Christ's wild
ambitious halo, scraped up now
in patches—had anyone imagined before
how invisible light would play
across dark marble
and rendered that imagining
through a loom algorithm with
dozens of workers: how the cost
of that great artifice
would be a human face that barely

holds as one?
For years
I was jealous of the people
who could fall asleep instantly
in Christ's lap, hands
inherently folding. But Christ
doesn't even hug John here:
it's more like he's about to decide
what gesture to make, what chord
to play. The most expressive
hands in tapestry
say almost nothing. There's nothing
natural to say,
only choices, which build
up beneath the heddles like static
electricity between wool and silk, sparking in the gilt.
Everyone knows it's impossible
to make God correctly beautiful and human
so why not gold
for bread and wine? Cissubstantiation's
desperate. There's foot washing
or healing in the back
and a hotel server wears the only shoes

in a foreground full of remarkable feet,
which is how you can catch the real
betrayer stepping
over his seat, purse
bulging like garlic, his right
foot's sole
soft and also bulbous. The orange
shirt is confirmation. Most everyone
twists away from disfigured Christ
but only Judas turns toward him
while walking away, stripped of the halo: no
art. His knife stays behind, pointing
at the problem. Namely, no
human contains their justification.
The grail sits in a bowl
to catch the excess blood.
The barkeep keeps pouring, non-
disciple. He looks rather wealthy
so perhaps he is us. Keep
the world coming, dredge it up.

In Practice

In the forests of Pannonia the birds
had feathers that shone together
like flames in the unvisited
Hercynian wood of Germany we've heard reports
of species of winged things whose plumes
light up in the nights in the manner
of fire in the prairie where
the Hoocagra lived the pale-leaf helianthus
lead a rainbow of grasses
in the legend of a single world of all
the times the great
imperial city of Vienna
rules Pannonia reborn with two
swans implausibly floating
in the Wien outside the walls a prairie
palette bleeding
in their necks a river
where reflection honors line
erases color
though one can run there today
past giant videos marketeering
human faces and flames
like Hersinian

birds that in the moment of Vienna
Pannonie seem frankly
less revivable: why not choose swans
I often wonder whether paper then
was white for on the prairie
under smoke from the distant
bay where the Amah Mutsun lived
in autumn 2020 there's no whiteness
but in the mąkąwirirotapanah which
in practice go a little hued
as if to say "for 'lived'
please read 'still live'" in 1493
when this woodcut was assembled
pressed and bound
so neatly as an opening
in the *Liber chronicarum* no one
in Vienna knew that Ottomans
would come thirty-six years later
to those fields
with armies of dechristianed
men how did the Ho-Chunk know
in 1760s French accounts
about the ocean

where the sun sets the Christians
so anxious to fix
the truth to scatter it
they had to stamp out words
on flattened cloth and trees
I resist bad scholar listening
in the long afterlife
of displacement murder slaving
and their kids as if
there were learning without harm

                                            but what

I've learned is one
all time-things exist unbound
collucent in us
and in the world
accessible by labor at all points and two
what's happened changes
and endures changes so endures endures
and changes in the transitive
especially on fragile nomad paper
so in Wolgemut's workshop's towers of Wien

the sacrality of towers is
a spatial cipher for the awe
of time or when a city
skyline rides the prairie
and sandhill cranes write spindly
legs in the haze do not
misunderstand the sun do not
misunderstand the flowers

Carpaccio's Ten Thousand Soldiers Betrayed by Their Generals and Sent to Asia to Die

I've never been able to tell you what kind of distance I have
when I bring you into a painting
and how much it matters what you want and what I give,
what kind of warm twilight you want to inhabit,
and whether you're next to me or with me at all.
I want to fold the scene into our gentle resistance
all summer long, at moments the a/c
coughing shut

and then you hear the storm and its pellets
and you look outside: an important tree
has broken in two, its many angles of branch
remembering darkly

                    the pink
lightning in a Giorgione sky and below
while thousands of people are dying alone their dying
is shared: if you're with me

this is the moment I realize the model for this and any European painting
of ten thousand martyrs would be the plague: where else
would you get all these bodies with feeling?

The workshop modelbook figures from former masters
for the suffering of Christ and his follower victims
will remind you since thirteen forty-eight no Venetian
had ever expelled the plague from their eyes.
That time I said "don't believe in suffering"
I wasn't denying the plague in your eyes.
I was trying to be honest about heaven,
where to find the knees when composing a body that failed
or the point of ascension on a swirling hill,
how paltry that portal has to be
and how magnificent the angels,
more gatekeepers than guides
and terribly beautiful. The original
workers' compensation
is the sight of bounty
attiring the agents who keep it away.
I meant: "don't take what they're offering."

Invocation: Jan Brueghel's *Harbor Scene with Christ Preaching*

Jan quotes his father with the proverb
that big fish eat the small ones, as if
to say he was or wasn't
eaten by the past. But some of us
want to be eaten. The bird
in the upper right
looks like a Stymphalian
monster, unangel. Not from here. The glare

on the pic in Larry Silver
makes it hard to see
whether the break in the clouds is just
expensive paper. How many people on the shore
want to be misled, want a strong
voice to take strong teeth and wrap
a wet mouth over them? Not

Christ. It's mainly the painter who believes — even
when trying to escape, which Jan
is not — in the power of transmission: but
without exception in time
iconography turns into grief, recognition into desire
to decipher. To unwind

the turbans in the middle ground, unshuck
the oysters, make a stand
about context. That stocky pier in the corner's
not a column, and I can't determine
the world. There's a rope around a trunk, but the whole point
is it doesn't
lead to anything for sure, slacks
into ground, doesn't
have the tension you'd expect
from a warship. It's almost funny

that these painters
in all their wars and plagues
were mostly unworried we'd lose the thread, requiring
the goofy art
historians to slap
each other's graspy hands. But I'm
not laughing. I have wanted an end
because I've wanted a different
beginning. Now I'm on the invisible dune

looking down on this shore and waiting
for it to come in, that beginning,

the one that gives assignments
in the wake of all this death,
says the war is over, organizes
shipments, distributes the fish,
which cannot quote the dead
alone. Piled next to the empty shells
that always also mean pilgrim, profit, empire,
dear Fish, please
keep stinking of the sea
when the story is retold.

Primordial Tide Pool

End Game

The land started peeling
up off the burning
mantle, which hissed, and as
the land peeled it translated
itself into a symbolic order
deliberately unintelligible
to anyone who had tasted it.
Available only to aliens
and the radically young
it flew in a difficult direction
so they could see it, a sweet
game. This is what became

of us, once the land was done.
Not we ourselves but the important
turns among us
transformed into non-player characters,
new scapes of fractal antigrids.
Atemporal beats. Sometimes
especially beloved animals
come up as conditional
parameters for the kind of play
that happens instead of story.

I'm sorry I go
no further than this.
The save points
trend line.

Self Portrait in a Primordial Tide Pool

I am standing at the interface of every
body of water I've loved
on a low jut of land. On my head

is a giant keychain, with the lumpy
rusty sieves I've collected
dangling, clanging. This is the hour

I announce, autumn. I got here early,
bad church tower. I'm covered
in slurs, graffiti, scratches, my forehead says

IM A SHIP OF THESEUS
STAN in dotted red
scabs. But it's my chin that weirdly

keeps getting longer. It droops now
into the sea, and when I talk
it walks on the ancient bed, trawling

coelacanths. I am a coward: I never
get in, never taste the ocean any
more, just stand there and let

the bottom of my face and top of my neck
droop into deep history, the other scale
of time. Jennifer, I miss swimming

but my name isn't Jennifer. What
will keep the smell in the air,
the specific leaves fermenting here,

crunching there, on the small
place I remember as land? I'll
persuade it to stay with my mumblous

humming and recitatives, feet
thumping. Slow run. *Original*
means originifying but

it should mean love
with nowhere to go but in
and out. The sun slinks south.

The Relief

Relief is knowing agency
isn't just effect and fault.

A clatter under small crystal,
a winter stream, the freedom

to wander, err. Finally, repetition
means control and desire

together. The ground leaves in the yard
wink in tandem from old rain

and the air leaves hover
over what they've done, cells

preparing to digest their own
chlorophyll. It was summer

around the cave when the fire
made the story, when the shadow

asked to be permanent.
Birds never ask this. They

cannot say it, but their existence
relies on never naming spring.

The Relentless Production

When I arrived at last in Jericho, the rival
KFC and Popeyes
lots were full
a few blocks from the cakey
winter homes. I re-rig the cable cars
to the mountain of temptation
Helena needed for the first
colonization in the name of Christ
and tell the handsome
young engineer
the oldest and terriblest prophecy.

I am in a hurry to stay in the present
and alive. My guide's body hates, head
down, arms pointed, lips preparing
spit: despite it I insist
on looking at the next excavation. Should I not,
if it is inevitable, oversee
the relentless production of caves
and redistribute the enemy's shekels?
The waiter corrects me. I must try
to find the souk or at least

the hidden equipment
for harvest. Rows of stumpy
date trees float in the salt lake.

My Mark of the Beast / Poem about the Octopus

The thing we know about nature
is it's already free. Wrung from it
all laws are baby rubrics,
finger puppets dressed like cops
for the abstract infractions
of capital. What I can tell you

about second nature is it's more
intractable than the first: it's logic's
toxic friend. The helicopter
attempts innocence, suburban
calm, lawnmower of the sky,
blower of infoliate clouds, while we

do not quite riot, singing
about Palestine. Information poses
as a cure to fear, but feeds it. Hope
feeds on beauty, but, addict, needs
more and more. I want to unsee
how quickly suffering breeds it,

beauty, how totally harm befunds
the beauty that builds tolerance

of harm, that even pushes worship
of its pathos. Jennie says we can
go hiking. I think of the hills outside
the suburbs west of Jerusalem,

walking at dusk to the columbarium,
passing beneath the rock onto its floor
and thinking as it opened
its perforated violet mouth
that doves lived there, not ashes.
Do we have to be melancholy

about revolution in 2024?
The helicopter stays. Blood
thumps in the ears, but if you try
to talk to it you die. Imagine
propaganda so powerful two
thousand years later a child

of people born eight thousand
miles apart an average of twelve
thousand miles away is forced
to learn the empire's language.

Not only that, I loved it, until
I learned to fetishize the language

the Romans themselves fetishized.
I call to Gaius in my dream
at the Asian fusion restaurant
and impress him with my Greek
poem about the octopus. It climbs
up the generative pre-trained walls

that were just barely holding
against the rising sea. "I will be
extinct now," one of us screams.
The papers say amnesia
is president of the Philippines.
The copter turned into a pop-up show

of art. I miss the stupid octopus,
but I can be its legal heir
only outside the empire.
I am trusting it to find our home
beyond the reasonable horizon.
Beneath these clothes I bear its mark.

Its Different Laws
for Nadia Chana

Nadia, have you ever tried singing
to your writing? Its different laws
like rivers, not even laws—a sense
that nothing is artificial
and our agency, while capable
of fault, also flows—only your voice
in your deep space
can bring those patterns
back. And your voice
is never alone, because of time, because
of all the suffering yous who have wanted
to wrestle with the wrongs of meaning,
the historical twist and our discontinuous
ways of being with the land, how to be honest
if not right, from the outside. You are
a chorus of wrestling moves and obstacles.
The song of them is a radical love.

In/firmation

I have come with a hammer to streets of glass

The great stores are under active armed guard

Don't you feel ghosts in the water humming

~~If something stops improving must've been abandoned~~ lol

Have you tasted rust when watching a train

Squeal dust, honest friction, a limit you can feel

Other shapes of the world inside the world

Turn over slowly in low boil, gymnastic

I know the guards get me in the end

Tropes swing like trapezes in the chat

Personless and airless, though dark mode

Is still brighter than a body: I wish

We really could shoot rays with our eyes

We really could hear a loved one's sonar

The kinetic record obscure to the wrist

So Grateful I Turn to the Art

When uncertainty became a sheaf
of probabilities, and those formulas crept
inside us, I went every day to the water

and watched it

lose its underhair
to a kind of lake combine (a water
harvester) or lap lap light
at its prairie banks, which nodded back
a very sleepy rainbow, blazing stars purple
and brown, big bluestems blue-green
and brown, compass plants green-yellow
and brown, purple coneflower orange-
and-brown-hearted, all set

in a tall
grass
three-dimensional matting
waving at the clouds: are you measurable,
I asked, have you been approximated, does it
matter, is your matter in any
meaningful way repeated in the numbers, and

will you decline somehow, measured,
does the wild seem weaker now, how can I
fight for you, what innocence must I push
into to find you again

trembling at every scale, a wind
that could include people
blowing at every scale, reciprocal twitching.
A great cluster of ducks appeared in the bay,
hundreds. Sandhill cranes
stalked the path. Above art installations
eagles spread and contracted, their wingspans
changing as they whirled
closer, lower, farther, past
the treeline, hungry and
enjoying hunger. Every time I'm in a high

place I stop for the eagles, hawks, falcons,
vultures, etc., even sometimes buzzards, not
to identify them in the moment,
who would want to, lords of the only metaphor
that helps, sharing our infringements — I
stop between trees or in the field
and look up like I'm in a copy

of a painting of Icarus where Icarus
wins and onlookers know it, wind
on my teeth, whistling again
through my rictus. This is it, the innocence
of technology: I thank the golden eagle,
who laughs back at biomimetics.
It knows the article where we marvel
how smart its use of wind, how complex
our mappings. Awkward. I am
so grateful I turn to the art

installation and get banging: I take the sticks
and strike the pipes, the one rhythm
I know. I'm feeding it math. I've
sacrificed family. I've sacrificed community.
I'm so sacred the only thing left
is the altar, which is this, wherever
you see me: assume I'm guarding the altar
that guards itself. Thank you,

water. Thank you, buildings.
Thank you, aquatic weed
harvester, slimy greens sliding
up your mouth the way the moon
slides up the frame of a window.

The Siege

When does the great fortress
become beautiful, or how, I wanted
to investigate. But no one
had survived the war.

I wanted to understand
how information undoes beauty
and v. v. So I am coming
to your fortress sharing walls

with a sea enhanced
by livestreamed reels of refugees.
I am coming to your fiction
of the tomb of Alexander

and letting down my vanished hair.
The water like a hostess rises.

De re metallica

Today I woke up haunted by the man
playing the US national anthem
on the ancient bone flute
in that Herzog film. This

is what I get for not having a past,
like a landscape painting in the early
sixteenth century. Everyone who sees me
wants to know where the humans are

and the answer is I'm a forest
with a few signs of habitation
and undirected danger like a smile.

Why can't I be claimed
by something coherent but not evil?
I tell the ghost I don't believe
a message can be universal.

This exorcism fails. He sits on my bed
watching my rivers pretend to be fountains.
We debug an app that beautifies
the mines inside my mountains.

At Last the Archive

Our world is still the world that requires displacement
and the isolation of variables, though

at last the archive creeps
back up the strings, a sparkly
residue. The sparks stand in for potential
activation. But soft.

A machine left on the gentle setting
so it would last forever. . . .

I'll save you the trouble. On the other side
of the quest for the flaming swords
it's a library, not a garden, now.
It grew fat over the years
from the minerals in the killers'
children's tears.

On the Way to the Paintings of Forest Robberies

Gender and the future
approach together, the monster
of time and construction
as loss. It hasn't worked
to battle grief by refusing it
so I'm back to Benjamin
and the syllables that fall
into meaning, the tragedy game:
just be, just be, no pressure.
Let being and making
be the fullest
forms of grief. On the way
to the paintings of forest robberies
raccoons rise up from nothing
into my lights
like grid modernity feralized.
On the other side the city
commemorates thefts over centuries
in those warbled mini
skyscraper eyes on the lake.
Believing we can listen
can be the closest thing
to listening, and change
life. Like humility, eating

the wiggly morphemes that move
sentience from sense. So
sing to me, city, whatever,
on this weedy lake, wherever,
algal bloom like rot
sputtering in anyone's lungs.
There's no one better
to talk about genitals
or the evacuation of specifics
in a fantasy of being true
to pleasure in one's body
than the end, Big Friend,
horizon. Our big friend horizon
or ocean in which we're suspended
or sun in whose unruly magnet realm
we spin, or galaxy, etc., night,
lets us confuse presence
for distributed intelligence
as long as we want. So there is
no first or last. I'm choosing
the ice cream sold at the best
conclave of the common. Why
not. There is no direction.
Eat and shout.

On First Looking into Me I Got Some Savonarola

A wall came out of the world.
Like in a film by Stanley Kubrick
where he wants to show the monster.
But here the monster is the end.
I bet you thought I'd say
the monster is you.
It isn't. Your monstrosity is a vain
fight against the monster monster.
Or more the fight
never to see the monster
or smell it. What does the end
even smell like. It smells
as much like petrichor as you'd expect. Except
there is no smell
and there is no rain. No rain but a rain
that breaks the pavement.
A marathon of rains. An ultra
ultramarathon. The worst thing is the wall
doesn't have a face. It makes you think
it has a face. You orient yourself to it
by feeling a face confronting you.
Confronting me. Contra me.
My crime. My crimeliness.

But there is no mei deus.
There is no miserere.
Only incidentally
is there unhappy ego.

Meanwhile

there are hangings
and even burnings still.
They knock on the wall.
That's what you hear.
Tap tap tap, tap tap tap.
The fucked-up echo of abundance.
We are doors in the wall.
We are optional doors.
When we choose to open
we could say miracle.
Reorientation. A terrible gas,
the atmosphere
to which we open. We get to say who breathes it.
What a glory. Which I have prepared.
For those who love thee.
Here the echo of abundance.

Acknowledgements

Some of these poems have been published, sometimes in different forms, in *ALL Review, Cul-de-sac of Blood, Fence, Here Magazine,* the *New York Times Magazine, Panda's Friend,* and *Spirit Duplicator.* I am grateful to Christine Kanownik for being the first reader of many of these poems, to Sharon DeGraw for her work on the cover and layout, and to the editors of *Fence* for their considerable help.

Also by Jennifer Nelson

Aim at the Centaur Stealing Your Wife

Civilization Makes Me Lonely

Disharmony of the Spheres: The Europe of Holbein's Ambassadors

Harm Eden

Lucas Cranach: From German Myth to Reformation

The Ottoline Prize

Tina Brown Celona *The Real Moon of Poetry & Other Poems*

Rosemary Griggs *Sky Girl*

Harmony Holiday *Negro League Baseball*

Lesle Lewis *Rainy Days on the Farm*

Kaisa Ullsvik Miller *Unspoiled Air*

Chelsey Minnis *Zirconia*

Lauren Shufran *Inter Arma*

Josie Sigler *Living Must Bury*

Laura Sims *Practice, Restraint*

Ariana Reines *The Cow*

Beth Roberts *Like You*

Kim Rosenfield *Phantom Captain*

Sasha Steensen *A Magic Book*

Stacy Szymaszek *Journal of Ugly Sites and Other Journals*

Wendy Xu *Phrasis*

Elizabeth Marie Young *Aim Straight at the Fountain and Press Vaporize*